Penguin

DYNASTIES: PAINTED WOLVES

STEPHEN MOSS

LEVEL

ADAPTED BY NICK BULLARD
SERIES EDITOR: SORREL PITTS

PENGUIN BOOKS

UK | USA | Canada | Ireland | Australia
India | New Zealand | South Africa

Penguin Books is part of the Penguin Random House group of companies
whose addresses can be found at global.penguinrandomhouse.com.
www.penguin.co.uk www.puffin.co.uk www.ladybird.co.uk

Penguin
Random House
UK

BBC Dynasties: Painted Wolves first published by BBC Books, an imprint of Ebury Publishing, 2018
This Penguin Readers edition published by Penguin Books Ltd, 2021
001

Original text written by Stephen Moss
Text for Penguin Readers edition adapted by Nick Bullard
Text copyright © Stephen Moss, 2018
Cover image copyright © Nick Lyons, 2018

Photo credits
All © copyright Nick Lyon except:
page 5 (hyena) copyright © Jurgens Potgieter/Shutterstock.com;
page 6 (break) copyright © jannoon028/Shutterstock.com;
pages 24, 27, 28, 29, 30, 31 and 32 copyright © BBC; page 38 (lions) copyright © Simon Blakeney

The moral right of the original author has been asserted

Printed in China

The authorized representative in the EEA is Penguin Random House Ireland,
Morrison Chambers, 32 Nassau Street, Dublin D02 YH68.

A CIP catalogue record for this book is available from the British Library

ISBN: 978–0–241–52063–5

The original book was published to accompany the television series
entitled *BBC Dynasties* first broadcast on BBC One in 2018.
Executive producer: **Mike Gunton**
Series producer: **Rupert Barrington**

All correspondence to:
Penguin Books
Penguin Random House Children's
One Embassy Gardens, 8 Viaduct Gardens,
London SW11 7BW

Contents

Animals in the book

painted wolf

lion

elephant

impala

baboon

hyena

New words

bite

break

chase

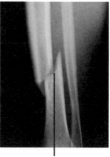
pup

fight

film crew

hole

smell

Note about the book

In 2018, the BBC showed the TV programme *Dynasties* about animal families across the world. They went to the Mana Pools National Park in Zimbabwe and **filmed*** a family of painted wolves.

In wolf families, the children often have to move away from home. Sometimes the children are not happy with their parents, and sometimes there are **fights**.

David Attenborough works with the BBC. His TV programmes about animals are very famous in Britain and the world. In *Dynasties*, he tells the story of Tait, Blacktip and their family.

David Attenborough

Before-reading questions

1 What do you know about wolves? Think about these questions:
   - Which countries do they live in?
   - Do they live together?
   - What do they eat?
2 Read the "Note about the book". Answer these questions:
   - What is the TV programme *Dynasties* about?
   - Where did they film the painted wolves?
   - Do you know David Attenborough's TV programmes? Which programmes do you know?

*Definitions of words in **bold** can be found in the glossary on pages 63–64.

CHAPTER ONE

Tait's pack

This is Mana Pools National Park. It is in Zimbabwe, near the Zambezi River. The park is home to a lot of different animals. Sometimes the park is rainy, and sometimes it is **dry**. Many animals come to the river and drink the water.

Mana Pools National Park

Tait is the **leader** of this pack of painted wolves.
They live in Mana Pools National Park.

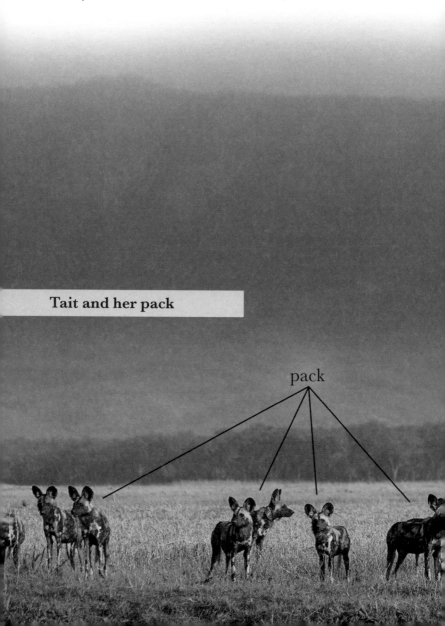

Tait and her pack

pack

The leader of a pack of painted wolves is always a **female**. There are about fifteen wolves in the pack. Many of them are Tait's children.

painted wolf

This is Tait and her daughter, Tait Junior.
Tait is nine years old. She is an old wolf.

Tait (left) and Tait Junior (right)

CHAPTER TWO

Tait's daughters

There are three wolf packs in Mana Pools. The packs have their own **territories**, and Tait's pack has territory near the river. There is food all year.

Two more wolf packs live near Tait. The leaders of these packs are Tait's daughters, Janet and Blacktip.

A lion

Some lions have territory between Tait and Janet. Lions do not like painted wolves, and they often kill them. The wolves do not usually go into the lions' territory.

Blacktip's pack lives next to Tait. Blacktip's pack is big. There are thirty wolves, but their territory is small. They do not have much food.

Painted wolf children do not usually **fight** their mothers, but Blacktip's pack needs food.

Blacktip's pack

One morning, Tait's pack **smells** something in the wind. It is Blacktip's **smell**.

Blacktip and her pack are running into Tait's territory, and they are ready to fight. Tait and her pack fight for some minutes, but Blacktip has more wolves with her.

Blacktip's pack moves into Tait's territory.

Tait's pack crosses the river.

Tait and her pack run away across a river.
Blacktip does not **chase** them.

Now Tait's pack is in the lions' territory. There are twenty-six lions here. Can the wolves stay here?

CHAPTER THREE

Filming the wolves

It was **difficult** to **film** painted wolves. For nine months of the year, they moved every day. Their territory was about 400–600 square **kilometres**.

Filming the pack

It was never easy, but people from Zimbabwe helped the camera **crew**. They found the wolves for them. The camera crew **followed** the wolves for 669 days.

In the rainy months the rivers were very big, and the wolves moved into the trees. It was difficult for the camera crew, because the **ground** was wet.

Filming elephants

The camera crew filmed different animals in Mana Pools, too. Sometimes they were very close to them.

CHAPTER FOUR

Hunting impala

There are elephants in Blacktip's new territory. Painted wolves do not hunt elephants because they are too big.

Elephants watching Blacktip's pack

Elephants do not like painted wolves, and sometimes they chase them.

Hunting impala

Blacktip's pack needs a lot of food. Painted wolves usually hunt in the early morning or the early evening. They often hunt impala. The pack walks slowly and gets near some impala. The wolves **choose** one animal and chase it.

Painted wolves can run at 65–70 kilometres an hour, and they can run for hours. Impala can run fast, too, but they get tired. In this hunt, Blacktip runs next to an impala and **bites** its back leg. Then, more wolves jump on the impala, and the hunt finishes.

After the hunt

In the rainy months, painted wolf packs usually kill two or more impala a day. Some days, Blacktip's pack kills six impala.

Blacktip's pack eating an impala in the evening

CHAPTER FIVE

Hunting baboons

In the dry months, it is not easy to hunt impala. The pack must find different animals for food. Painted wolves do not usually hunt baboons, but there are a lot of baboons in Mana Pools.

A baboon

Baboons come down for food.

Baboons are very big animals. They sleep in the trees, and the wolves cannot get them there. But in the day, the baboons come down from the trees. They are looking for food.

The baboons are on the ground, and the wolves move slowly between the trees. Their heads are down because they are hunting.

Ready to kill

The baboons see the wolves and they run. But then, the big **male** baboons turn and chase some of the wolves.

There is a big **fight**, and there are too many wolves in the pack. But baboons can bite, and many of the wolves are **hurt**.

A male baboon

After a long fight, the wolves kill a young
baboon. Now the pack can eat.

Blacktip has five pups. The pups live in a **hole** in the ground – a den.

Wolf pups

Blacktip is hunting, but some wolves stay and watch the pups. The pups play on the ground near their den. The wolves watch and listen for lions.

Watching the pups

34

CHAPTER SIX

Living with lions

Tait's pack now has new territory, but there is
not a lot of food. There is danger from lions,
too. But the pack finds food, and Tait makes a
new den near the Sand River.

Lions are always a danger.

Tait's den is in a good place. She can see the river, and she can watch for danger from lions or **hyenas**.

Near the new den

Tait and a male wolf, Ox, have two pups at the new den. Ox sees his pups, and he is happy. The wolves in Tait's pack are happy, too.

Ox meets his pups.

Lions sometimes chase the wolves. One **female** wolf, Wicket, **breaks** her leg and cannot run. The pack stays near Wicket and **looks after** her.

CHAPTER SEVEN

Blacktip and the hyenas

The next months are very dry. Blacktip and her pack move near the Zambezi River because they need water.

There is not a lot of water.

At first, Blacktip looks after her five pups all day. But after some weeks she can go away from her den in the day.

One day, Blacktip smells something on the ground. It is an old smell, but it is her mother's. She knows it well. Blacktip can follow the smell and find her mother, Tait.

Blacktip, with her pack and her pups, follows the smell. They are going into lion territory and into danger.

Blacktip and the pack travel all night. But tonight, the danger does not come from lions. It comes from hyenas.

Travelling at night

Blacktip's pack goes into lion territory.

Hyenas usually hunt at night. And tonight, they are hunting Blacktip's pups. There are fifteen hyenas, and Blacktip's pack turns and fights them. The camera crew has night cameras. They can film in the dark.

The pack runs at the hyenas.

The fight is long, but the hyenas kill one of Blacktip's pups. Then, the hyenas run away with the **dead** pup, and the wolves are not happy. But Blacktip does not stop. She is following Tait's smell.

The hyenas kill a wolf pup.

Tait is at her den in lion territory. Then, on the wind, her pack smells something. Blacktip and her pack are coming. But Blacktip's pack stops by the river. There is now only a kilometre between Blacktip and Tait. It is now morning.

By the river

Now, some lions are moving near to Blacktip's pack. The pack is in danger.

Blacktip and her pack turn back from the lions and the river. They run all day and all night for 25 kilometres. The next morning, the pack is at home in its territory.

CHAPTER EIGHT
Home again

Tait and her pack cannot smell Blacktip. They are not in danger from Blacktip now, and maybe they can go home. But Tait does not go home. She is very old now, and after ten days she dies.

The pack needs a new leader. For some weeks there is no leader, but then the pack chooses Wicket. Wicket cannot run very well because her leg hurts. But she is very intelligent, and this is important for a pack.

The pack's territory

Wicket leads the pack to its old territory. She has pups now, but one day a hyena kills her. The pack needs a new leader again, and it chooses Tait's young daughter, Tammy.

Tammy (top left) and her sister Twiza (right)

Some **males** from Blacktip's pack come into Tammy's pack. Then Tammy has seven pups. Now there are twenty-three wolves in her pack. Blacktip has more pups. She now has ten. But the two packs do not fight.

Blacktip and her pups

CHAPTER NINE

The future

What is the **future** for painted wolves? Today, there are about 400 packs with about 4,000 wolves in **southern** Africa.

Painted wolves are in danger. Lions kill a lot of wolves, but people kill them, too. There is good news in Mana Pools because there are more wolves now. Tait is dead, but she had many children, and her children had many more pups. In Zimbabwe today, there are 280 wolves from Tait's family.

During-reading questions

CHAPTER ONE

1 Is Mana Pools rainy or dry?
2 Who is Tait?
3 How old is Tait?

CHAPTER TWO

1 How many wolf packs are there in Mana Pools?
2 What animals have territory between Tait and Janet?
3 Why does Blacktip's pack go into Tait's territory?

CHAPTER THREE

1 Why was it difficult to film the painted wolves?
2 How many days did the crew follow the wolves?
3 What did the wolves do in the rainy months?

CHAPTER FOUR

1 Do painted wolves hunt elephants? Why/Why not?
2 When do painted wolves usually hunt?
3 How many impala do the wolves kill in a day?

CHAPTER FIVE

1 What do these painted wolves hunt in the dry months?
2 How many pups does Blacktip have?
3 Where do the pups live?

CHAPTER SIX

1 What can Tait see from her new den?
2 How many pups does Tait have? Who is the father?

CHAPTER SEVEN

1 Why does the pack move near the Zambezi River?
2 What does Blacktip smell?
3 What are the hyenas hunting?

CHAPTER EIGHT

1 Does Tait go home?
2 What kills Wicket?
3 Do Tammy's pack and Blacktip's pack fight?

CHAPTER NINE

1 How many painted wolf packs are there today?
2 How many wolves are there from Tait's family?

After-reading questions

1 Look back at your answers to "Before-reading question 1".
   Were you right?

2 What did you learn about the painted wolf packs in
   Mana Pools? How big are they, and who are their leaders?

3 Territory is important for painted wolves. Why?

4 What are the dangers for painted wolves?

Exercises

1 Write the correct word in your notebook.

dry	fight	territory	chase	smell	leader

1 ....*dry*........... not raining

2 .... a very important wolf

3 .... A family of animals lives here. Other animals cannot go there.

4 .... You hit someone and they hit you.

5 .... You do this with your nose. Animals can do it very well.

6 .... to run behind a person or animal

2 Write questions for these answers in your notebook.

1 *Who is the leader of the pack?*

Tait is the leader of the pack.

2 There are about fifteen wolves in the pack.

3 The pack's territory is near the river.

4 Tait smells Blacktip.

5 They run across a river.

6 They are in the lions' territory.

3 **Complete these sentences in your notebook, using the words from the box.**

followed	difficult	kilometres	film
	ground	crew	

1 It was ...._difficult_............ to .... painted wolves.
2 Their territory was about 400–600 square ....
3 People from Zimbabwe helped the camera ....
4 They .... the wolves for 669 days.
5 It was difficult because the .... was wet.

4 **Write the correct verbs in your notebook.**
1 Painted wolves do not _**hunt**_ / **hunted** elephants.
2 Elephants do not **like** / **likes** painted wolves.
3 The wolves **choose** / **chooses** one impala and **chase** / **chases** it.
4 Painted wolves **can running** / **can run** for hours.
5 Blacktip **run** / **runs** next to an impala and **bite** / **bites** its back leg.
6 Painted wolf packs usually **kill** / **kills** two or more impala a day.
7 Some days, Blacktip's pack **kill** / **kills** six impala.

5 **Are these sentences *true* or *false*? Write the correct answers in your notebook.**

1 Painted wolves usually hunt baboons. ....*false*..........

2 Baboons are very big animals.

3 Baboons sleep on the ground.

4 The wolves' heads are down because they are tired.

5 Many of the wolves are hurt.

6 Blacktip's pups live in a tree.

6 **Complete these sentences in your notebook, using the words from the box.**

lions	hyenas	dens	baboons	fight	pups
	hurt	male	female		

1 ....*Baboons*......... are big animals. They live in trees.

2 The baboons .... the painted wolves, and many wolves are ....

3 Young wolves are ...., and they live in ....

4 .... and .... are dangerous animals for painted wolves.

5 A wolf mother is a ...., and the father is a ....

7 **Look at the picture on page 43, and answer the questions in your notebook.**

1 What are these animals?

They are hyenas.

2 When do they usually hunt?

3 How many are there in the pack?

4 What are they hunting?

5 Who is filming them?

6 What do the hyenas kill?

7 Are the wolves happy?

CHAPTER EIGHT

8 **Put these sentences in the correct order in your notebook.**

a .... A hyena kills Wicket.

b .... Blacktip has more pups.

c .... Some males from Blacktip's pack come into Tammy's pack.

d ...*1*.... Tait and the pack cannot smell Blacktip.

e .... Tait dies.

f .... Tammy is the new leader.

g .... Wicket is the new leader.

h .... Wicket leads the pack to its old territory.

9 Correct these sentences in your notebook.

1 Tait goes home.

  Tait does not go home.

2 Tait is very young.

3 Wicket can run very well.

4 A lion kills Wicket.

5 Blacktip and Tammy's packs fight.

6 There are 400 wolves in southern Africa.

7 People don't kill wolves.

8 Tait didn't have many children.

Project work

1 You want to film the painted wolves. Write a letter to the Zimbabwean people in a village near Mana Pools. Ask for their help.

2 You are filming one of the wolf packs for one day. Write a diary page about the day.

3 You filmed the fight between the wolves and the baboons or between the wolves and the hyenas. Tell a friend about it. Write the conversation.

4 Make a poster about painted wolves, or a poster about another animal in danger.

An answer key for all questions and exercises can be found at **www.penguinreaders.co.uk**

Glossary

bite (v.)
A dog can *bite* you with its mouth. Then you are *hurt*.

break (v.)
You *break* your leg. You cannot walk.

chase (v.)
to run behind a person or animal. You try to catch it.

choose (v.)
You can have this thing or that thing. You must *choose*.

crew (n.)
These people do a job together.

dead (adj.)
not living

difficult (adj.)
not easy

dry (adj.)
not raining

female (n. and adj.)
a sex. A woman and a girl are *females*. Animals can also be *female*.

fight (n. and v.)
You hit someone and they hit you. This is a *fight*.

film (v.)
to take moving pictures with a camera

follow (v.)
to walk or run behind a person or animal

future (n.)
the time after now (tomorrow, next week, next year)

ground (n.)
The *ground* is under your feet. You stand on it.

hole (n.)
a place in the *ground*. Some animals live in a *hole* under the *ground*.

hurt (adj.)
You have an accident and then you are *hurt*.

hyena (n.)
A *hyena* is an animal. *Hyenas* kill wolves.

kilometre (n.)
You can run a *kilometre* in about six minutes. A *kilometre* is 1000 metres.

leader (n.)
The *leader* is a very important wolf. All the other wolves *follow* their *leader*.

look after (phr. v.)
to help a person, animal or thing

male (adj. and n.)
a sex. A man and a boy are *males*. Animals can also be *male*.

smell (v. and n.)
You *smell* things with your nose. Animals can *smell* things very well. They can *smell* the *smell* of another animal. Then they *chase* it.

southern (adj.)
Countries in *southern* Africa are Zambia, Zimbabwe, Botswana and South Africa, for example.

territory (n.)
A family of animals has its own *territory*. The family lives there and other animals cannot go there.